From the Authors of *Lifeonaire* and the *Companion Study Guide*

TRANSFORM YOUR MARRIAGE VISION RETREAT

a self-guided getaway for couples

STEVE & MICHELEEN COOK

Transform Your Marriage Vision Retreat: A Self-Guided Getaway for Couples

Copyright ©2021 by Steve Cook and Micheleen Cook. All rights reserved.

Published by Lifeonaire Publishing, LLC
9111 Cross Park Drive
Suite D-200
Knoxville, TN 37923

www.lifeonaire.com

No part of this publication may be reproduced, stored in a retrieval system or transmitted in any way by any means, electronic, mechanical, photocopy, recording or otherwise without the prior permission of the author except as provided by USA copyright law.

Book Creation and Design
DHBonner Virtual Solutions, LLC
www.dhbonner.net

ISBN: 978-1-7330423-1-4

Printed in the United States of America

Table of Contents

Welcome to the Lifeonaire Marriage Vision Retreat vi

What are the Benefits of a Marriage Vision Retreat? ix

Pre-retreat Exercises xi

Suggested Schedule for your Retreat xv

Introduction xix

CHAPTER 1: Getting the Most out of Your Marriage Vision Retreat 1

CHAPTER 2: Communication: the Foundation of a Successful Retreat 5

CHAPTER 3: The Mission of your Marriage 9

CHAPTER 4: Getting Started on your Marriage Vision: Vision Elements 13

CHAPTER 5: Marriage Vision Writing 25

CHAPTER 6: Celebration is Important! 29

CHAPTER 7: Streamline Your Vision 31

CHAPTER 8: Taking Action 35

CHAPTER 9: Build Accountability 37

Conclusion 39

Appendix 41

Sample Parenting Plan 44

Marriage Vision Element Worksheet 46

PRE-RETREAT

*Do this prior
to your retreat!*

Welcome to the Lifeonaire Marriage Vision Retreat

Dear friend,

"Is there a secret to a great marriage?" I actually enjoy asking older couples what is that one secret they can share which has helped them to have a long and healthy marriage. Some of the responses are intended to be funny, like "Always assume she is right" or "Tell him he did a great job and fix it after he leaves." On a more serious note, I am commonly told things such as "Don't go to sleep angry," "Always work things out," or "Make sure you talk things through." At the end of the day, all of these answers boil down to one thing: communication.

I have come to realize that communication is the key to a successful marriage! However, many couples struggle to really communicate with each other daily. They love each other very much, but they don't take the time to understand one another. Instead, many assume that because they love one another and have some things in common, they will always be on the same page when making foundational decisions for their marriage and family. This assumption is a trap that keeps couples stuck in conflict — they don't know how to work through differing desires and opinions (that they assumed would never be there). Instead of growing together, layers of hurt, wounds, and scars from unresolved conflict begin to build up and undermine the hopes and dreams of the marriage.

At Lifeonaire, we have walked individuals through the process of creating a vision for their life at our "Get-a-Life" events — in addition to individual lives being transformed, we have seen marriages reinvigorated and begin to flourish when couples work together on their visions. Consequently, for several years, I have wanted to offer a resource to help couples improve their marriages. My wife and I put together this self-guided Marriage retreat using the Lifeonaire vision writing process that has already benefited many marriages. We believe that your marriage can experience the same breakthroughs! Before you start your retreat, make sure to take time to complete the Pre-Retreat Exercises.

Blessings,
Steve Cook
Founder of Lifeonaire

What are the Benefits of a Marriage Vision Retreat?

1. It is all about your marriage:

This may be the first time you have ever taken time like this to plan the way you will spend your life together. You get to set the time, date, place, and events for your retreat. You get to set the stage, be creative, and dream with your spouse. You get to decide how much time and energy you invest into your vision planning sessions. You, as a couple, get to take charge and create a vision that will guide your marriage and give you direction that will pay benefits for years to come.

2. You get on the same page — using the power of vision:

The Marriage Vision Retreat will help you to build a vision for your marriage. A marriage vision is a written description of what your ideal marriage looks like; it is your template, blueprint, or roadmap that you use to create your own unique marriage. It will serve as your guide and reference so that you can determine whether your choices and actions are moving you closer or further away from the marriage you want to live. A written vision brings clarity and unity. It is a powerful tool in your marriage — it is your playbook.

3. Enhanced communication:

At your Marriage Vision Retreat, you will be asked to discuss foundational elements in your marriage, which provides an opportunity to really listen to, understand, and learn about your spouse. You may begin to appreciate things about them that you never did before, and the moments for emotional intimacy are great! You will also have the chance to work through areas that have caused conflict rather than avoid it. There is nothing more empowering in a relationship than working through and achieving a solution in an area that previously divided you. This experience has great potential to grow trust and confidence in one another. Through open and honest communication, you will find yourselves drawing closer to one another.

4. An opportunity to reconnect:

You are alone with your spouse — no electronics, no kids, no work. Your Marriage Vision Retreat carves out time to make some new memories and have fun together. It also gives you space to be physically and emotionally intimate without being interrupted. What more could you ask for!

Pre-retreat Exercises

"A great marriage doesn't happen because of the love you had in the beginning, but how well you continue building love until the end."
–unknown

A Marriage Vision Retreat is an exciting time for you and your spouse to get away and work on your marriage vision together. It is time that you and your spouse intentionally set aside for just the two of you to connect, date, dream, and have fun together. Having a shared vision is going to lead to incredible things in your future. When you got married, you and your spouse joined the same team, but just because you are on the same team does not mean you were on the same page.

The purpose of this retreat is to get the two of you as a couple, as teammates, playing from the same playbook. You will become a unified team using the same playbook — your marriage vision — to move forward into the best marriage you can have. Here are a few quick exercises that you should do before your retreat to make the most of your time together:

Pre-retreat exercise #1: Set a date and make arrangements.

This should be an event that is just between you and your spouse — no kids, no other couples, just the two of you (Exception: Other couples are welcome if you are attending an organized Marriage Vision Retreat for couples). Plan on getting away for at least three days, do more if you can. There are no set rules on where you should go for your Marriage Vision Retreat. It doesn't have to be far away or expensive, but it does need to be conducive to being together and alone. So whether you choose to go camping, stay at the Ritz Carlton, rent an Airbnb, or stay at the Holiday Inn around the block, the key is to get away.

If this is your first Marriage Vision Retreat, it may take you longer to write your original marriage vision. However, if you already have a marriage vision written, each retreat will be a tune-up and may not require as much work time.

Pre-retreat exercise #2: Pick the Vision Elements that are most important to you.

During your retreat, you will be given suggested elements of a marriage vision to discuss with your spouse. This list is not inclusive of all elements; however, you should each review the list below prior to the retreat and pick the two or three most important ones to you individually.

Now, the intent of this retreat is not for you to go through all of these elements, but we certainly want you to go through the ones that are most important to you. Remember, there may be other things that are more important to you — this is your marriage, and our list contains suggestions, which might be all you need. Don't feel like you can't add to it; this is to help you get the process started.

- Charity and Serving
- Conflict Resolution
- Family
- Finances
- Fun and Laughter- Dating
- Health
- Hobbies
- Holidays
- Parenting
- Roles in the marriage
- Schedules
- Sex Life/Expectations
- Spirituality
- Technology
- Work

His Top 3

1. _____
2. _____
3. _____

Her Top 3

1. _____
2. _____
3. _____

Pre-retreat exercise #3: Commit before leaving on the retreat to work through any uncomfortable issues that arise and to do so in a positive way.

Your time with your spouse will be fun, and you have something to look forward to together. For some of you, the idea of this seems uncomfortable. Like all marriages, you probably have struggles or conflict that is not being dealt with. More importantly, it feels like whenever you talk about hard things, conflict comes into the picture. So you would rather avoid it. We are here to tell you that there should be some hard things discussed during this retreat. Conflict is a part of every relationship, and it is not bad if handled correctly. Conflict, when handled well, leads to stronger relationships and growth.

Additionally, you may have never done anything like this before. Vision writing is a new concept for many people. You should allow each other room to be comfortable with thinking small as well as big. For example, it is not easy for a mother with kids at home to think beyond being a mother. The only vision many mothers can see in the moment is to make sure the kids survive one more day. Give room for that to be OK. If you are in a place where you can't see beyond right now, use this time to focus on how you can be the best you can be with the life you've been blessed with at this moment.

Pre-retreat exercise #4: Write an appreciation letter for your spouse.

Everyone loves feeling appreciated, so your next exercise is to write out an appreciation letter for your spouse! Take your time with this and think of everything you can — include all of the things you appreciate about them, not just the big things but also the little things. (Be sure to take this with you to your retreat as you will use this several times.) If you want to go all out, you can put it in a card or, better yet, make a card.

If you need some help with this, start by mentioning all the things you first loved about your spouse, and then move on to talking about all the things you have come to learn about them and what you appreciate about them now. Finally, mention all that you look forward to.

*Watch video: Preparing for Your Marriage Retreat
Video links can be found in the appendix

Here is a helpful checklist for preparing:

Item	Check
Set a date	
Book a hotel room	
Take time off work	
Arrange for a babysitter	
Arrange for a pet sitter	
Make a packing list 1. Journal 2. Appreciation List for your spouse 3. Device for watching retreat videos 4. Bible (if desired) 5. Calendar 6. 7. 8. 9. 10.	

Setting a Schedule

Get excited! Planning your retreat schedule ahead of time will make your time together more relaxed and productive. Consider such things as planning to work during times when you are both most productive (morning, mid-day, or night) and doing something fun together during the "not so productive" times. This is your time away from all responsibility, so we also highly encourage you to incorporate romantic time into the retreat schedule each day . . . enjoy one another, make lots of love, eat good food, be active, have more sex. You get the idea!

Suggested Schedule for your Retreat

A sample schedule for Day 1:	A sample schedule for Day 2: "morning thinkers":	A sample schedule for Day 3:
- Check-in - Pray - Share your appreciation list - Read: Chapter 1 and 2 - Read: Chapter 3 - Marriage mission exercise - 30-minute break - Read: Chapter 4 - Read: Chapter 5 - Marriage vision element exercise - Read Chapter 6 - Date night	- Breakfast - Prayer/ Devotions - Share your appreciation list - Review chapter 2, 4, and 5 - Marriage vision element exercise - Break for lunch - Marriage vision element exercises - Date night *If you are a "night thinker", have your date activity in the morning and start on your marriage vision element exercises after lunch.	- Breakfast - Prayer/ Devotions - Share your appreciation list - Read: Chapter 7 - Review and Double Check exercise - Write a Pocket vision exercise - 30-minute break - Read Chapter 8 - Put it on the calendar exercise - Read Chapter 9 - Build accountability exercises - Read Conclusion - Celebration Lunch

Your Marriage Vision Retreat Begins Now!

*From here on out, you should read this workbook together.
Get close, take turns reading, and have fun!*

Introduction

*"A good marriage isn't something that just happens;
you have to work it, and you have to keep on working at it."*
-Steve Cook

WE WANT TO CONGRATULATE you for taking this step. Not only will your marriage benefit from going through this process, but the time together should be FUN! Plan on having fun; it will be the two of you alone, away for a couple of days. We challenge you to date again and to dream again! You are spending the next couple of days with the most valuable player of your team. Make the most of it and enjoy!

This workbook will help you develop a marriage vision together through a self-guided Marriage Vision Retreat. The goal of writing a marriage vision during a retreat is to get the two of you on the same page regarding the essential areas of life. Having a marriage vision will help you stay on the same page as you experience life's inevitable changes. As your kids grow older, their needs and activities change, and how you interact with them changes. As you each grow older, your bodies change, your needs and desires change, but you are still on the same team. With time, the playbook of the past will need to be updated, and the more often you do it, the better off you will be. So, revisiting your vision is critical because having a Marriage Vision Retreat once a year is one of the most valuable things you can do for your marriage — keeping your marriage vision fresh and relevant is key! Not only will it be a great time of getting away and investing in your most important relationship, but it will help you to communicate important things in life that change over time.

*Watch video: Remember to Pursue Joy
Video links can be found in the appendix

Getting the Most out of Your Marriage Vision Retreat

1. Participate fully and have fun: Eliminate all distractions and fully immerse yourself in your retreat. Be present in all ways (mentally, emotionally, spiritually, and physically). Listen and carefully watch the videos with your spouse. Think deeply about the subjects and discuss them honestly. Turn off your cellphones/electronics when not watching a retreat video and stop thinking about your to-do-list back home. Be here now and enjoy it. You are in for a fantastic few days!

2. Approach this with a heart of understanding: Take the time to understand your spouse's perspective, and this will go a long way. Be open to your spouse's thoughts, opinions, and ideas. Be open-minded and don't automatically reject them. Let them simmer for a bit and ponder whether they could be true and how they could apply to your marriage. Be honest. It is easy to look for faults in what your spouse says and reasons why what he or she suggests will not work. This will kill intimacy, discussion, and progress. In areas of disagreement, you are both likely right; you are just different in the way that you see things. Commit to understanding and not quitting until you find common ground and common solutions that you both are satisfied with.

3. Take action and complete all the exercises. You will get out of your retreat what you put into it. Take lots of notes and capture as many ideas as you can. Once the retreat is over, take action immediately. Take the next steps together to implement the marriage vision you wrote. The longer you wait, the less likely you will make meaningful changes in your marriage.

On a spiritual note: There is no doubt that you can create a very good marriage by getting on the same page and implementing your marriage vision through your Marriage Vision Retreat. However, if you want to experience the absolute best marriage that you can have, look to the one who created marriage for guidance in writing your marriage vision. God's playbook, the Bible, gives directions on how to have a Godly marriage. Another recommended supplementary resource to the Bible in creating a Godly marriage vision is Visionary Marriage by Dr. Rob and Amy Rienow.

Let's discuss some ground rules before you jump in:

This needs to be a safe place. You both may hear things that you don't like, but it will never come out if you are not committed to hearing your spouse. You should resolve upfront to listen to the things your spouse has to say, and let them get it out on the table. You need to get the hard things on the table. Commit to understanding your spouse's perspective before reacting defensively.

Listen. Be prepared to listen to your spouse. Learn the technique of reflecting on what your spouse is saying to make sure you understand. You must listen to one another during this time. We get so busy in our day-to-day world that we often forget to slow down and listen to what our spouse is really saying.

Commit to Having Hard Conversations (if need be). The process required to write a marriage vision hinges on your commitment to have hard conversations, if they come up, while discussing fundamental areas of your marriage. It is much better for your marriage if you have hard conversations rather than to avoid them and let it get in the way of you having the best marriage you can have. Let us encourage you to push through. This is something that will transform your relationship. Communication is key!

Have the right attitude. Become Mr. and Mrs. Right — the most important part about this is for you to become the right person. As you go into this retreat, take some time to think about who you need to become to be Mr. or Mrs. Right for your spouse. Be committed to making the changes.

Keep it simple. This is intended to be simple, not complicated. We want you to be successful with it. At the end of this retreat, we want couples to walk away with a clearer understanding of their mission for marriage, their roles in the marriage, and a playbook on how to carry it out.

Pray together. Take the time to pray with one another each day before and during the retreat. Ask God to show the two of you what he wants for your marriage. Consider what values you want your family to be known for. Some examples may be: servanthood, loving, charitable, respectful, etc. Ask God to help you incorporate these values into your vision. If you find yourselves stuck in a hard conversation, ask God to bring you both to a place of understanding, humility, and resolution. Pray that God will come in and be part of this time, pray for guidance. If you enter into this with the right heart and seek God, you will come out of this better than you started.

> Prayer example: *God we thank you so much for this marriage. We are so blessed to have each other. As we start our retreat today, Lord, we pray for your guidance. We invite your presence throughout this retreat. We put every activity unto your hands; we pray that you will guide us. Please put a hedge of protection around our time, our marriage, our conversations, our health, and our family back home. May nothing come against us during this retreat. In Jesus' name we pray, Amen.*

Have fun. Take as many fun breaks as is necessary to keep you both working towards the same goal of writing your marriage vision. Some exercises require more time and communication. Whenever one or both spouse(s) is feeling mentally or emotionally fatigued, take a break. Have fun, but commit to returning to finish the exercises that day. Lastly, you are alone. Yes, part of your time together should be enjoying one another sexually! This is an important part of your relationship. Look forward to it!

Communication: the Foundation of a Successful Retreat

*"The greatest marriages are built on teamwork... a mutual respect,
a healthy dose of admiration and a never ending portion of love and grace"*
—Fawn Weaver

THIS MARRIAGE VISION RETREAT workbook will give you a structure to help you to constructively work through topics that may never get discussed or are only discussed in the heat of disagreement. This book is not intended to be a fix for each and every problem that a couple deals with in their marriage; however, it is intended to provide you with the tools, time, and space to discover what you both want for your marriage moving forward and to put it into a plan of action.

Communication Tips

Communication can be fantastic or tricky. It is much more than just the words you use — it is also facial expression, body language, attitude, and meaning conveyed. Although it is common for most individuals to learn to speak words as a toddler, the art of communication does not necessarily come naturally; it requires learning and practice. Consequently, improving your communication skills is a sure way to take your marriage to the next level. Let's face it, great communication is fundamental to a great marriage. Here are a few tips for better communication during your retreat:

- Your spouse will be more honest, authentic, and intimate in conversation when you signal that he or she is valuable and what he or she is saying is worth your full attention. So switch off all technology e.g phones, laptops, and television during your retreat conversations (unless you are watching a retreat video together).

- Be specific. Generalizations or absolutes (like "You always…" or "You never…") are rarely true and such phrases will elicit a defensive and resentful stance from your spouse. Understanding and cooperation is rarely achieved when one spouse feels like he/she needs to defend him or herself against "untruths" being spoken.

- Use "I" instead of "You" phrases. You can state your needs or desires in a way that is less likely to elicit defensive feelings in your spouse by using "I" statements. For example, "I wish you could see how much I do at home for this family" is stating your desire for acknowledgment. In contrast, "You don't see how much I do at home for this family" is pointing out the failure of your spouse to acknowledge you.

- Learn how to express negative feelings constructively. It is impossible to have intimacy with your spouse if you are harboring negative feelings. While these feelings need to be communicated to elicit change, you can learn to express them constructively. Do you see the difference in these statements?: "I am disappointed that you took extra shifts at work." compared to "Clearly you don't care one bit about me or the children. You keep on working late every day."

- Learn to listen to your spouse without getting defensive. If you find your defenses going up, take a deep breath, and ask yourself questions before responding: "Is all or part of what he or she is saying true or feasible?", "Why is this making me defensive?", "What part is my pride, fear, or need for control playing into my reaction?" Be honest about your feelings and take responsibility for them.

- Ask questions for clarification rather than make assumptions. It is very empowering when someone works to really understand what you are thinking or saying.

- Make positive expressions. Most people are quick to express negative feelings more often than positive ones. Ensure you are expressing gratitude, adoration, respect, and admiration to your partner. Your spouse will pay more attention to your grievances if your compliments exceed complaints. Be sure to read your appreciation list (that you wrote before the retreat) to your spouse each day during your retreat.

*Watch video: Having Hard Conversations
Video links can be found in the appendix

RETREAT EXERCISE #1

Read your appreciation list to your spouse now.
Start every retreat day with reading your appreciation list to your spouse. Feel free to add to it as you learn new things about your spouse during the retreat.

The Mission of your Marriage

AT A LIFEONAIRE GET-A-LIFE event, we begin the vision writing process by helping individuals determine their values and, to a certain extent, their mission for life. These values are important to recognize so that they can be incorporated into the vision. So, before you dive into writing your marriage vision, it is important to answer the question: "What is the mission of my marriage?" Then, you can incorporate that into a Mission Statement for your marriage.

Is this a challenging question for you? We bet it is! Most couples have difficulty answering this question as they have never really thought about a mission for their marriage. Some may say that the mission of their marriage is to be together and stop there. Others may say that the mission of their marriage is to love and care for each other. Still, others will say, "I don't know, I was just attracted to my spouse, and we thought it was a good idea." If you are a Christian, the Bible provides much guidance on the biblical purpose for marriage — it just about lays out a mission statement.

A marriage mission statement is a statement of why you are married and the purpose behind it. Having a marriage mission statement enables you to have meaningful direction in marriage rather than aimlessly wandering through married life. In addition to providing direction, it elicits what values you allow to guide your marriage. When you have a clear mission for your marriage, you can hold each other accountable to the shared direction and values portrayed in that mission. Your marriage mission statement will also largely shape your children's understanding of marriage and provide a marriage guide to the next generation as they watch you make decisions based on your purpose and values. An example of a mission statement for a Christian marriage might be: *To raise a family that knows and loves Jesus Christ.*

Once you determine your marriage's mission, you can better articulate what you desire out of your marriage. So before you go any further, take some time to discuss the mission of your marriage. Do your best to put it into words. We understand that this can be difficult, but you need to spend some time on it (not a lot). You do want to get to the vision writing part, but this can serve as a foundation for building the rest of your vision. Know that whatever statement you come up with, it should be compelling, unifying, and bring passion into the marriage.

*Watch video: Developing a Marriage Mission Statement: Having a Purpose for your Marriage
Video links can be found in the appendix

RETREAT EXERCISE# 2:

Discuss the mission of your marriage and write a mission statement.
If you need help with formulating your thoughts, consider the following supplemental questions. (These are the same questions we use at our Lifeonaire Get-A-Life events to help attendees get in touch with who they really are and to determine their values.)

Supplement Question A: What do I desire out of my marriage?

Supplement Question B: Suppose you have three months to live; what would that look like? What would you do? How would you spend your time?

Supplement Question C: Children's lives: What do you want your children's lives to look like? How do you want them to experience life? Think of every aspect of their lives.

Supplement Question D: Write your eulogy. What would you like the person giving your eulogy to say about you? Write what people would say about you if you died today. Be honest with yourself as much as you can. Compare what you would like them to say to what they would actually say. This will allow you to check whether you are on the right path or need to make adjustments in your life.

Design it, Frame it, Hang it

One cool thing that others have suggested is to take your mission statement, have it designed into a nice picture, get it framed, and hang it in a prominent place in your home. This not only is something to serve as a reminder of what your marriage is about, but it is also there for your children and others to see.

Getting Started on your Marriage Vision: Vision Elements

THERE ARE MANY ASPECTS to our marriage. Some are more pressing than others, and the importance of each of these in your life will change over time. For the purpose of this exercise we refer to these as *vision elements*. Vision elements are high-level categories, parts, or segments of typical marriages. Each listed vision element is meant only as a suggestion — not a set-in-stone requirement. They are meant to guide you into meaningful discussion on those elements that need the most attention at this point in your marriage.

As you read through the following section, consider which elements you would most like to focus on during your retreat. You had an opportunity to review these prior to the retreat and you should each have a list of your top 2-3 areas that you would like to address.

*Watch video: Marriage Vision Elements
Video links can be found in the appendix

RETREAT EXERCISE #3

Read through the Marriage Vision Elements.

Roles in the marriage

Many couples never discuss what they believe the role of each spouse should be in marriage. They simply make assumptions about what role their spouse will play in their marriage based on what they saw in the marriages around them growing up. However, your spouse may have grown up in a type of family in which roles in the marriage were defined differently than your experience. You can see the potential for major conflict! Frustration results when those (often unspoken) assumptions or expectations are not met.

Let's get one thing straight: You are both valuable to your marriage.

- Take some time to discuss the gifts and talents you each possess. Recognize, celebrate, and nurture them.
- How can you define roles in your marriage that best utilizes each spouse's strengths?
- Consider how this translates into practical tasks like distribution of household daily chores, child care, handling of household finances, handling of home maintenance issues, spiritual leadership, etc.

If you are interested, the Bible has a lot to say about roles in marriage as God designed it. Do you know the roles that God intended for each of you? We would also highly recommend reading "Visionary Marriage" by Rob and Amy Rienow if your goal is to live a God-centered marriage.

Work

At a Lifeonaire Get-A-Life event, we help individuals develop a life vision similar to what you are doing with your marriage vision. This requires significant thought given to the lifestyle one desires to live and why he/she chooses the lifestyle he/she does.

As part of writing a marriage vision, It is important to think through the lifestyle you both desire to live and its ramifications on your marriage. You have an opportunity to live a simple life or a complicated one (meaning living a life of always pursuing more). When you choose to pursue a complicated lifestyle, you usually have to work more. Oftentimes, it requires both a husband and wife to remain gainfully employed with no hiccups to maintain the lifestyle from a financial perspective. Unfortunately, the pursuit of such a lifestyle means sacrificing in other areas. While such a lifestyle may cost a lot financially, what else does it cost you? How much time are you giving away? How are your relationships? Has it hurt your marriage?

Most marriages start out with two incomes, and along with that comes the lifestyle. Once kids are introduced into the picture, life becomes more complicated. Motherly instincts kick in, but the financial ability to be a stay-at-home mother has been compromised because of the lifestyle the couple chose early on. This is one of the leading causes of conflict in a marriage. The burden on the husband to sustain a lifestyle once supported by two incomes by himself puts a lot of stress and pressure on the marriage. I (Steve) once wrote an article on the blessings of a single income household. When you can learn to live off of one income, life is much simpler. Lifestyle choice is yours, but it needs to be a mutual decision that should be revisited often. At Lifeonaire we highly encourage you to consider designing your lifestyle around a single income. The freedom you have will be far greater, and it comes with unexplainable joy and peace. If a second income is introduced into a lifestyle (that can be supported by one income), then you will be blessed in many ways.

Contemplate such questions as:

- Who is the primary breadwinner? Do you prefer to have 1 or 2 incomes?
- Work outside the home vs stay at home vs a hybrid of both?
- How many hours do you want to spend at work?
- Issues related to travel for work?
- Childcare issues and work?

Finances

Arguments about finances hamper many marriages. According to a survey assessed by Family Relations in 2020, financial problems are the leading cause of divorce today. There are several aspects to consider when discussing financial issues with your spouse.

- Are financial decisions made by one party or both of you?
- Are bank accounts joint or separate?
- Who handles paying the bills and managing bank accounts?
- Are you on the same page about charitable giving?
- Are you on the same page in regards to college funding?
- How do you handle debts?
- How do you handle credit card spending?
- Are you on the same page about investing and retirement planning?
- Do you both feel good about the answers to the above questions?
- If not, what are the objections or concerns

Parenting

Honestly, this one element could be a retreat unto itself. You do not need to solve every parenting issue with this one retreat, but pick one or two issues in which changes could improve your marriage relationship and have the discussion. Little steps will add up to big results. Aspects of your parenting vision will change as children grow from infant, toddler, adolescence, teenager, college, adult children, to grandchildren. Consider your goals for parenting and what theories guide your parenting decisions: biblical or secular.

- Are you satisfied with the direction that your family is going? If not, what needs to change?
- Are you making parenting decisions that seem right or what is easy at the moment? (Think about when your children grow up and are 25 years old, what would they say about your parenting decisions looking back?)
- How do you distribute daily parenting duties in each stage of development?
- What is your method of discipline? Are any changes in philosophy necessary for discipline?
- Evaluate how you communicate with each child. What works and what does not? Are changes needed?
- How do you handle technology?
- Extracurricular schedules?
- Transportation?
- Allowance and savings for the future?
- Blended families will have additional issues that should not be pushed aside. Being on the same page in parenting is the best thing for your entire family to function in harmony and unity.

As children move through stages of development, so must the parenting portion of your marriage vision in order to address new needs and challenges. In addition, no two children are the same. Therefore, you need to have a parental plan that is flexible enough to cover the individual needs and challenges of each child. One thing that you can do during your retreat is to recognize the uniqueness of each child and to write a letter to each child. Recognize each child's love language, gifts, talents, and special abilities. Consider how you can nurture each child in a way that is meaningful to him or her. These letters will be treasured possessions to children for years to come.

See the sample parenting plan in the appendix.

Sex Life expectations

Sex was designed by God to be a beautiful thing experienced between a husband and wife. It is also one of those topics that many are uncomfortable talking about. How will you ever develop a better understanding of sex within the context of your marriage if you do not discuss it? Now is the time.

When a couple does not understand one another's needs, expectations, or views about sex, then it leads to a lot of frustration and hurt feelings. Let me be vulnerable for a minute: My wife and I, like many couples, have struggled in this area. What we have discovered, as we have sought to understand one another, is that we both like sex. However, we like it for different reasons. We also have different needs. My wife doesn't think about sex during the day, like I do. She sees it as a way to connect, but for her the intimacy of connecting is what makes her feel loved. I also see it as a way to connect, but the act of love making is what makes me feel loved. Physically, it does not take much for me to be ready to go. My wife's body takes longer to be physically ready.

Neither of us are wrong, we are just different. However, if I expect her to see and experience sex the way that I do, I judge her needs and actions in the wrong light. And vice versa! I might feel like she doesn't love me when she takes longer to respond. She may feel like I don't love her and that all I want her for is sex. It has taken a lot of honest communication for us to come to understand our similarities and differences in the way we feel loved as it pertains to sex. We have found the book <u>31 Days to Great Sex: Love, Friendship Fun</u> by Sheila Ray Gregoire to be a great resource in sparking conversations in this area of our marriage.

During your retreat, if there are struggles in this part of your marriage, spend time hearing each other out and understanding what the other desires.

- What are your honest views, expectations, and needs about sex?
- Is your desire for your sex life different than what it really is?
- What needs to change to fulfill both of your needs in this area?
- What do you like and dislike about sex?
- How often would you desire to have sex?
- When do you like to have sex? Is there a special time of day?
- Is sex a challenge? What makes sex a challenge?
- What sexual baggage needs to be dealt with?

The more honest and understanding you can be, the greater chance for intimacy to grow. It is worth it!

Spirituality

We, personally, believe that marriage is an institution that was created by God. He created a woman (Eve) from a man (Adam) so that the two could be joined together. Looking from the perspective that God is the head of marriage and that he created the two of you to be together, may prompt you to view your spiritual life as more important to your married life than before. Take some time to discuss the importance of spirituality in your marriage moving forward. A few questions to help you with your discussion include:

- If you could have the ideal spiritual life as a couple, what would that look like?
- Do you share the same beliefs?
- Who is the spiritual leader in your home?
- How does the church fit in to your marriage?
- Do you, or will you pray together?
- Will you do devotions together? With your family?
- Will you surround yourselves with like minded people via a small group? Or through serving?

Holidays

We each grow up celebrating holidays and special occasions differently in our families of origin. Some families go all out and others are more reserved. Expectation (often unspoken) can really put a damper on the holiday mood and cause conflict in your marriage. Schedules and traditions are just a few areas that can bring much joy or cause much strain. I (Micheleen) remember listening to a couple at a marriage retreat lament how stressful holidays were for them. Each set of in-laws put so much pressure on the couple to attend extended family gatherings that they found themselves a slave to the in-laws' calendars. They had no time to celebrate together as their own family.

Differing view of technology during holiday gatherings was also a challenging issue for this couple. One spouse thought it was a waste of time to watch TV all day with her in-laws on Thanksgiving; she much preferred visiting and playing games like her family did. She admitted to having a bad attitude when going to her in-laws for the holidays. Discuss with your spouse what expectations you both have in celebrating holidays.

- What were your favorite traditions?
- What traditions would you like to carry into your marriage/family?
- What types of gifts do you want to give your children? (For instance, in our household we give stuff for Christmas and experiences for birthdays).
- What boundaries need to be set with in-laws to make time for your own family during holidays?
- What schedules and boundaries need to be set with ex-spouses around holiday visitation time?
- How can blended families make holidays special for every family member?

Hobbies: Personal growth vs common interests

When you married your spouse, you did not marry your clone. Hopefully you have some common interests that you share and enjoy together. However, you are also an individual with unique interests and giftings that don't disappear once you say "I do". Consider your individual interests: hobbies, coaching, civic government boards, church activities, school activities, non-profit community clubs, sports, or arts. A goal in marriage is to come to a mutual agreement about how much time and resources/finances each spouse spends pursuing his or her own interests.

- What are the common interests that you share?
- Do you both agree on how much time and/or resources you spend together on hobbies/activities?
- What are your individual interests?
- How would you like your spouse to support you in your interests?
- How can you support your spouse in their interests?
- Do you agree on how much time and money your spouse is spending pursuing his or her hobbies?
- Is there a good balance between personal growth and common interest?
- How is personal interest affecting the rest of the marriage?
- What changes would you like to see made?

Fun and laughter: Dating continues throughout marriage

The most committed and happy couples make it a habit to have fun and laugh together. After all, laughter may be considered the soundtrack of a happy marriage. One great way to spend time together as a couple is to schedule regular dates. We know a couple that goes out to eat every Monday night — rain or shine. They value time to reconnect as a couple and this is how they choose to spend it. Sometimes, time just opens up and you need to take advantage of it. For my wife and I, we will go to a coffee shop for a conversation. It's easy, doesn't require planning, and it is something that we both enjoy. Discuss what brings fun and laughter into your marriage.

- Take some time to make a list of date ideas that you would like to do together — they can be big or little. Also write a list of default date ideas that you can do without much notice or planning.
- If childcare is an issue, make a list of potential babysitters that you can call in a pinch.
- Discuss how often you would like to schedule dates and put it on the calendar.
- What common interests do you share?
- How can you connect around your shared interests?

Charity and serving

Nothing binds two people together more than a shared experience in which you bless someone else. Nothing teaches humility, selflessness, and generosity to children like including them in giving to others. One way to leave a legacy to the next generation is to model service and charitable giving. Some of our best memories as a couple and as a family have been serving. I, Steve, like the idea of helping the needy, and I prefer to do it with food. I find great satisfaction in cooking or serving meals to others. I also enjoy serving this way, because it is easy for my kids to be involved, and I prefer to serve with my kids by my side. As a family, we like to go on mission trips. I (Steve) actually prefer mission trips to vacations. I can work really hard during a mission trip and come home refreshed. I tend to come home tired from my vacations. When we go on a mission trip as a family, we experience so much together physically, emotionally, mentally, and spiritually.

- Take time to discuss as a couple your interest in serving and charitable giving.
- What gifts or talents do you have that you can share with others?
- Do you prefer to serve individually, as a couple, or as family?
- What objections do you have towards serving or giving?
- How can you overcome current roadblocks preventing you from serving as a couple or family?
- What are some local ways that you can serve as a couple or a family?
- How often would you like to serve together?
- How can charitable giving fit into your financial budget?

Scheduling

Like finances, you make choices everyday about how you spend your time. Most of you will learn to juggle everything that is thrown at you, so the purpose of this exercise isn't necessarily to learn how to schedule all that is coming your way, but to schedule important things. We call these non-negotiable. Time together is important for emotional connection as a couple and as a family.

Dates and/or time participating in activities together as a couple are things that you may consider scheduling more regularly. As parents, you can also instill into your kids a value for family by setting regular family time together. For instance, our family has dinner together every night; sometimes it is early and sometimes it is late to make sure everyone is there. Of course, there are things that come up which make this impossible, but the norm is dinner together. Warning: scheduling gets more complicated as kids are introduced into the picture, as they get older, and as they take on more activities. Therefore, you may have to be more deliberate in scheduling the non-negotiables.

- Discuss what activities in your marriage and family that you consider non-negotiables. How are you doing in scheduling them into your daily, weekly, or monthly calendar?
- What changes need to happen to include your non-negotiables into your scheduling?

Conflict resolution

Every marriage has conflict. Conflict is healthy when it motivates understanding, personal growth, and positive change. Conflict is harmful when it is not dealt with- ignored or avoided to keep a false peace and/or there is constant fighting without any mutual resolution. Unresolved conflict can lead you to conclude that your spouse is your enemy. This is far from the truth.

Remember, when you got married, your spouse became your teammate. Teammates don't fight with each other; they fight side by side together to win the game. Instead of facing off, they come alongside one another to do battle. The battle is not between the two of you, it is against a greater enemy that wants to disrupt your marriage, put a wedge between the two of you, and permanently separate you. Don't fall for it! One of the biggest keys to conflict resolution is to listen and ask clarifying questions until you understand your spouse's perspective.

Take a few minutes and reflect on the *Having Hard Conversations* video where I (Steve) talked about perspectives (using the visual of a car accident. When the husband finally realized that his wife saw things differently, they came together. However, the wife also needed to realize that her husband was not wrong, what he saw was also true. He just had a different perspective).

Consider how you handle conflict in your marriage:

- As a couple, do you avoid or ignore difficult conversations to maintain the peace (even if it is a false peace)?
- Do you allow difficult conversations to escalate into name calling, accusation making, and finger pointing that ends with unresolved hurt feelings?
- Do you control conversations in such a way that your spouse does not feel part of the decision-making process?
- Do you come to a mutual understanding and mutually agreed upon solutions?
- Together commit to not avoiding or walking away from a difficult topic until you truly understand your spouse's perspective.
- If you are interested in learning new communication and conflict resolution skills together, here are a few suggestions: **1)** Read a book on communication together such as <u>Love & Respect</u> by Dr. Emerson Eggerichs, <u>Fight Fair: Winning at Conflict without Losing at Love</u> by Tim & Joy Downs, or <u>Keep Your Love On!: Connection, Communication, and Boundaries</u> by Danny Silk. **2)** Attend a marriage conference together. Local churches often host such retreats such as A Weekend to Remember. **3)** If need be, commit to finding a marriage counselor who can mediate as you work through issues that have become toxic in your marriage relationship.
- What other ways can you improve your marriage through better communication?

*<u>Re-Watch video: Having Hard Conversations</u>

Health

We have each been given one body to care for from birth to death. Micheleen's mom always said, "Buy good shoes because you will need your feet to last your entire life." What we do for our bodies today will affect it positively or negatively tomorrow, next week, next month, next year, and so on. This is one area you do not want to compromise, even though it is easy to make health less of a priority as life gets busy with marriage, family, and work responsibilities. Consider one change that you can make individually or as a couple in this area. Stick to it. Set some goals.

- How can you support one another in reaching and celebrating health goals?
- Are there health issues that you have put off until now?
- Make plans to begin to address it.
- Revisit the topic of health the next time you do a vision marriage retreat. This is one of those vision elements that changes with time.

Technology

Let's face it, technology and devices are a very real part of daily life. You can say that you wish you didn't have to use them, but more and more of the things that we do are requiring that we use a device. Unless you want to live completely off the grid, technology is becoming a necessity. I have come to realize that we can't just say that devices need to be shut off all the time. We can't tell our kids that they can't use them for long periods of time, because the moment we do, their school requires that an assignment be completed on one.

- What issues are technology causing in your marriage and/or parenting?
- How will devices not control your marriage?
- How will you put boundaries in place around technology use? What safeguards on devices do you want put in place?

RETREAT EXERCISE #4: Rank the vision elements together

Review and prioritize the marriage vision elements as a couple. Rank them from 1-13 on the importance of each to both of you. The most important to both should be #1. You will not have time to work through all the elements in one retreat. Focus on the top 3 or 4 elements between the two of you. Even if you only establish a vision for your #1 vision element, life will be much better. Ideally, it will be great if you work through 3 or 4 elements during this retreat. If you are having a hard time trying to figure out what should be #1, here is a hint: ladies first! Let her choose #1 and he can choose #2.

Number	Vision Element
1	
2	
3	
4	
5	
6	
7	
8	
9	
10	
11	
12	
13	

Marriage Vision Writing

A MARRIAGE VISION IS a written description of what your complete and ideal marriage looks like. It is your road map that you use to create your own unique marriage. It will serve as your guide and reference so that you can determine whether your choices and actions are moving you closer or farther away from the married life you want to live.

During the vision exercise, refrain from writing anything about money. You will have time to discuss finances, but remember this is a marriage vision, not a financial prospectus. Dream together! The following exercise may lead to some hard conversations and that is okay. If need be, go back and watch the *Having Hard Conversations* video again. Pray together for this time to be encouraging and for enhanced understanding and unity. Recommit as often as is necessary to fully work through this process. Remember that you are on the same team.

*Watch video: Essentials for Writing Your Marriage Vision
*Watch video: Tips for Writing Out Your Marriage Vision Elements
Video links can be found in the appendix

RETREAT EXERCISE #5

Starting with your top vision element (the one you prioritized as #1), you should individually take out a piece of paper and start to write. Follow the directions below. You should spend about 10-15 minutes on this exercise.

Write your vision around this element with no filters. Just write down everything that comes to mind. Do not filter what you write because of your current circumstances, situation, or environment. In this exercise you are looking forward to the life you desire to have. Be careful not to hold back because you think something isn't possible or reasonable. Maybe it isn't possible right now, but it should still be discussed. Do not edit, filter, or analyze your thoughts- just write what comes to mind. Remember there is no right or wrong answer.

RETREAT EXERCISE #6

Share with your spouse what you wrote.

Now is the time for you to really listen. Don't start giving your feedback or feelings without first understanding what your spouse has written. For example, if your spouse wants to move into a new home, don't interject with "I like our house, I don't want to move." You need to take the time to ask questions to understand why he or she wants to move into a new house. You may discover things that you didn't know. Oftentimes, when something is uncomfortable for one spouse, they will dismiss the desires of the other spouse. They make assumptions about motives.

On more than one occasion, I (Steve) have helped students work through a situation similar to the one above. The husband wants to move; he has dreams for his family; he wants what is best for his family. He thinks about it all the time. He doesn't dream apart from his family. His wife, on the other hand, is uncomfortable with his idea of moving. She says that she doesn't want to move without first asking him exploratory questions. He feels like his dream is killed because he was never given the opportunity to be fully heard or understood.

On the other hand, she may have in her vision — I love my house, and I want to live here for the rest of my life. He needs to take time to understand her reasoning as well. Perhaps there is a happy medium in the plan —like a second house. When you both truly understand one another, you may actually agree more with your spouse's vision than you would have originally thought.

Communication is so very important to this process. Take the time to listen and fully understand before reading or making conclusions. Once you understand each other, it is time to discuss and get the on the same page. Where did you agree? What gaps need to be closed? What would you like to see moving forward? How can you write a unified vision for this area of your marriage?

Write it down.

RETREAT EXERCISE #7

Record what you would like to see moving forward in this area- dreams, desires, needs or wants. Record any suggestions on how to move from where you are currently. Worksheets are located in the appendix.

Working through additional vision elements

Time permitting, repeat the same process you worked through for Element #1. Do this for as many of the elements that you have interest and time to work through.

Remember to eat and take fun breaks! We recommend taking a break between completing the exercises for each vision element.

TIPS: Don't let electronics creep in, be sure to keep them off. Take time to pray together. Read your appreciation list to one another, and perhaps add to it as you learn new things about your spouse.

Celebration is Important!

WEBSTER DICTIONARY DEFINES CELEBRATE as "to observe a notable occasion with festivities." In the article *The Importance of celebration*, Kathrine Spinney writes, "Celebrating allows us to take our minds off of the task at hand and focus on another important task on hand — recognition and appreciation for all that has been done."

You just wrote a marriage mission statement. You also took the first steps in creating your marriage vision for your top marriage elements. You dreamed! You had hard conversations! You potentially overcame mental and emotional barriers! You did a lot of hard work to get on the same page with your spouse! That is HUGE! That is worth celebrating! It is time to celebrate and have fun with one another. Get sexy!

RETREAT EXERCISE #7

Celebrate your accomplishments with a date night at the end of each day!

Streamline Your Vision

Review and Double-Check

Revisit what you wrote down for each vision element and do an honest self-examination to make sure that what you have is authentic and represents what you both really want your marriage to look like. Make sure that it feels right and isn't what you think you are "supposed to want." Ask yourself the following questions:

- Is it what I want?
- Is it true?
- Will it bring me more joy? Or will it weigh me down?
- Is this the right thing for us?
- Does it fit into our marriage mission?

Make adjustments if needed. Don't quit until both spouses understand, agree, and feel good about what is decided and recorded.

RETREAT EXERCISE #8

Review and make adjustments. Record any adjustments made.

Writing a Pocket Vision

Now that you have captured all the things you would like included in your marriage vision, it is important to simplify, clarify, and streamline it to make it more digestible. Moving forward from the retreat, you will want to review and read your vision with your spouse daily. You will be more likely to read your marriage vision daily if it is condensed. We call this your Pocket Marriage Vision and it is simply your longer vision condensed down to one page using a bullet point, short-sentence format.

*Watch video: Benefit of a Pocket Vision
Video links can be found in the appendix

RETREAT EXERCISE #9

Write a Pocket Marriage Vision

Take what you wrote in the previous long-form vision element exercises and do your best to succinctly state the main points from each section. These bullet point items are your vision element items. There are no rules as to what you write for your bullet points. They may be ways you feel, things you do, the experiences you have, or anything else you want to include in your marriage. Write out your bullet points for each vision element. A sample format is provided:

Pocket Marriage Vision

Vision Element #1:

- _____
- _____
- _____
- _____

Vision Element #2:

-
-
-
-

Vision Element #3:

-
-
-
-

Vision Element #4:

-
-
-
-

Taking Action

Putting It On the Calendar

This is your first action step. You have to make time in your schedule to carry out your vision if you really want to see progress. This is the perfect time for you as a couple to look at your calendars and schedule in what is important to you.

*Watch video: Prioritizing What's Important
Video links can be found in the appendix

RETREAT EXERCISE #10

When you look at your vision, there are a number of things that will take time. It is important that you take these items and put them on your calendar. Schedule them! Most of us will honor our calendar and follow through with the things that are already on our calendar. So go through your vision in priority order and put the most important things on your calendar, one at a time. Don't allow work or other things to get in the way of following through on these important issues.

Taking Action After the Retreat

You have spent considerable time and energy discussing and dreaming about your marriage. Don't let that go to waste. Once the retreat is over, take action immediately. Take the next steps together to implement the vision you wrote. The longer you wait, the less likely you will make meaningful changes in your marriage. Take action immediately!

RETREAT EXERCISE #11

Commit to reading your vision together daily. We encourage you to work reading your vision into your routine. Whether it is at bedtime, at the dinner table, or when you wake up in the morning, create consistent time for reading your vision together. Pray that God will lead you and help you move forward.

RETREAT EXERCISE #12

Make multiple copies of your vision, and put a copy anywhere you will see it daily: in your Bible/journal, purse/wallet, on your night table, bathroom mirror, etc.

Print out copies of your vision that you can carry with you wherever you go. I (Steve) keep one in my pocket, one with my to-do list, in my journal, in the book that I'm reading, etc… I take the time to read my vision as often as I can. It helps me to know when I may be getting off track and it gives me a reminder to make adjustments.

Build Accountability

YOU ARE NOW ARMED with a vision (your playbook) that will transform your marriage. The best athletes are not just given a playbook without someone overseeing them; there is a coach who holds the players accountable and keeps them working together as a team. Very few people can do this on their own. Do you need a coach? Not necessarily, but you will greatly improve your chances for success with accountability — be it a coach or by surrounding yourself with others who are on the same journey.

*Watch Video: Take Action
Video links can be found in the appendix

Post Retreat Exercise #1: Create a whiteboard

A whiteboard can be a very powerful tool for helping you to live and experience the vision that you have come up with. We can't take credit for this idea. It actually came from one of Steve's students. They took their key vision elements and posted the benchmarks that they wanted to hit on a whiteboard that they saw every day. The whiteboard was next to the door leading to their garage. Everyday, as they came in and out of their house, they were reminded of what they were pursuing as a couple and as a family. The reminder helped them to stay on track, and within a year's time, their marriage and family life was completely transformed. They are one of the most incredible couples we know today. They will freely share that they were on the verge of divorce prior to having a vision. Their vision, clearly in front of them everyday, helped them to stay on track and achieve great things.

Post Retreat Exercise #2: Communicate this with your kids, family members, and friends

Let them know the things you talked about and what changes they may see coming forward. Frame everything in a positive light and get their buy-in. As a quick note: You may not get total buy in from your kids. That is OK, but you still need to move forward and do what is right for your marriage.

If you are part of a small group, let them know what you have done. Share your marriage vision with them (the appropriate parts anyway). Just sharing your vision with others gives a degree of accountability. Finally, we would encourage you to share the vision writing process with others. I (Steve) find that when I want to grow in a particular area, the best way to do so is to teach it to others. It forces me to get better. You may not want to be the teacher, but if you are sharing the ideas and concepts with others, you will find that you are getting sharper with them yourself.

Post Retreat Exercise #3: Build community for accountability

Join the Lifeonaire community online and come alongside many like-minded people. Share your vision, your successes, and your challenges with the group, and they will come alongside you. You can simply download the Lifeonaire app or access it from your desktop.

You can also look for a Lifeonaire Connect Group near you that meets regularly (for a list of current groups, go to www.Lifeonaire.com). More groups are opening all the time, and great people are participating in them. If there isn't one near you, perhaps you can open one up.

If you really want to dive in, you can join a Lifeonaire Coaching group (go to www.Lifeonaire.com for more information) There is a financial investment to be a part of our Lifeonaire coaching groups; however, our coaching groups have proven time and time again to transform lives and businesses through helping our students implement their Lifeonaire visions. These coaching groups are mastermind groups, along with one-on-one coaching, that focus on both business and life.

Conclusion

WE ARE SO EXCITED for you! It is our hope that by taking this time together you have learned more about one another, you have drawn closer together, and you have become unified in areas of life that you may never have discussed before. Whether you read your vision every day or never again, the steps you took doing the exercises will be something that will begin to change your life. Following through with reading your vision every day and coming together to discuss it often will transform your marriage into the one that you dreamed about having when you first said "I do".

Marriage is a beautiful thing. It is not easy, but with work, it can be the most rewarding thing you ever experience. We believe that this retreat addresses many of the areas that create the biggest challenges for a marriage. You are now armed to conquer them together (as a team) and claim the victory that you deserve.

Appendix

Scan QR Code
or visit www.lifeonaire.com/mvrvideos
to locate all of the videos:

VIDEOS:

(1) Remembering to Pursue Joy

- Sometimes, not all teammates are on the same page (we're here to help you get on the same page)
- The American Dream can often distract from what we really want or cause us to believe
- Rather than focusing on what lifestyle you want, focus on what you want to experience and feel from your lifestyle

(1a) The Essentials for Writing Your Marriage Vision

(2) Preparing for Your Marriage Retreat

- Remembering your spouse is your number one
- Bring a journal if you need to
- Plan what you want to do on your retreat
- Be prepared to focus on one another
- Have fun!
- Watch the Hard Conversations video Pre-retreat
- Look at potential discussion items ahead of time, and pick your most important ones.

(3) Having Hard Conversations

- Listen with the intent of truly hearing what your spouse is saying
- Understand that you two may be seeing things differently, but that doesn't mean one of you is right and the other is wrong
- Talk about how you want things to be (ie, how you want to raise your kids, how you want to communicate)

(4) Developing a Marriage Mission Statement: Having a Purpose for Your Marriage

- If the purpose of your marriage is "Compatibility", you're on very shaky ground
- Your purpose will change everything

(5) Marriage Vision Elements

- There is no Right or Wrong way to do these; take these elements as suggestions
- Elements:
    - Roles
    - Work
    - Parenting
    - Finances
    - Faith
    - Personal Growth
    - Fun and Laughter
    - Serving and Charity
    - Schedules
    - Sex

- Conflict Resolution
- Health
  - Your Vision may change as life changes, and that's okay
  - Discuss these (or elements you come up with) and get on the same page with each one.

(6) Tips for Writing Out Your Marriage Vision Elements

- Do not filter anything
- Act like you're a kid at Christmastime
- There is no right or wrong Vision
- Write things in the present tense
- Focus on Positive not Negative

(7) The Benefits of a Pocket Vision

- Helps keep you and your spouse on the same page
- Is a great reminder of the plan
- Prevents distraction of what other people are doing
- Prevents you from trying to implement ideas without talking with your spouse first

(8) Prioritizing What's Important

- Anything that requires time should go on your calendar (i.e., Date Night)
- Prioritize life things first, not work things

(9) Take Action

- A Vision gets you moving in the right direction, so just start moving
- Print out several Pocket Visions and put them in places where you'll see them
- Ask for help in taking these steps and share your journey with others
- Surround yourself with likeminded people
- Implement "Whiteboard Warriors"
- Congratulations on getting started on this incredible journey!

Sample Parenting Plan

WE BELIEVE THAT IT is our responsibility to raise our children to know and love God. We are responsible for teaching them His ways. We will encourage them to seek out God's plan for their life and do everything we can to nurture them and help them to do so. We will do our best to grow and be the best parents that we can be.

Spiritual

- Daily devotions and prayer at dinner time
- Encourage our children to read their Bible- Bedtime routine
- Christian education (through high school)
- We are regular church attendees

Education

- Christian education for school
- Bible education at home on a regular basis
- Give them opportunities to pursue their own interests- let them fail
- Financial education, including giving and generosity
- Experiential education, travel and missions

Quality Time/Communication

- Eat dinner as a family consistently (prioritize)
  - Ask what their hardest thing and favorite thing were from the day
  - Devotion and prayer
- One-on-one trips on occasion with the kids
- Help them to grow and have a positive mindset
- Be present
- Stay active — sports

Discipline

- Limiting screen time – changes with age
- Learn to say I'm sorry the right way
- Consistent so they know the consequences
- Encourage boundaries and respecting them
- Remind them of what God expects and how he loves them
- Choose ways to discipline that are easy for us
- Both parents on the same page

Health (physical, emotional, social)

- Age-appropriate bed time
- Three healthy meals per day
- Encourage outdoor play at home and at school
- Annual doctor visits and dentist
- Encourage healthy snacks

Family Contributions

- Assigned chores
- Age-appropriate packing and unpacking for trips
- Keep room clean
- Help with yard work

Activities

- Sports/athletics, camps, science/technology not conflict with church
- Provide options for activities
- Should not interfere with education

Technology

- Age-appropriate limitations of technology for fun (30 minutes)
    - Earn by doing chores
- Up to two movies per week for a normal school week but not on a school night
    - Need to be earned by doing chores
- Age-appropriate use of cell phones

Marriage Vision Element Worksheet

Vision Element #_____:_____

Vision Element #_____:_____

Vision Element #_____:_____

Vision Element #_____:_____

Vision Element #_____:_____

Vision Element #_____:_____

Vision Element #_____:_____

Vision Element #_____:_____

www.ingramcontent.com/pod-product-compliance
Lightning Source LLC
Chambersburg PA
CBHW041103070526
44583CB00002B/37